ALL THINGS HAMSTERS FOR KIDS

FILLED WITH PLENTY OF FACTS, PHOTOS, AND FUN TO LEARN ALL ABOUT HAMSTERS

ANIMAL READS

THIS BOOK BELONGS TO...

____

____

WWW.ANIMALREADS.COM

CONTENTS

AN INTRODUCTION TO HAMSTERS

FURRY FUN FRIENDS

h, the wonderful world of hamsters!

Don't let their tiny size fool you—**these little balls of fur are packed with personality, and they'll keep you captivated and entertained for hours!** Hamsters are not only adorable, but they also make amazing pets for people of all ages.

Have you ever had pizza for dinner and wished you could save some for later, only you knew your siblings or friends would probably eat it first? If you were a hamster, you could save some extra pizza inside special pockets in your cheeks, and no one else could get it! Then, when you were ready to eat it, you could just take it out and have some slightly soggy pizza. *Yeah, that sounds pretty gross!* But this is exactly what hamsters do. They stuff their cheeks with food and then carry it back to their nest to enjoy it later. **Of course, nuts get less soggy than pizza does!**

As you join us on this hamster journey, you'll soon learn why so many people love them. With their cute faces and easily manageable care requirements, hamsters have quickly become a popular pet for many.

Let's explore the wide array of hamster breeds, learn about their diet and habits, and share some helpful tips on how to make these little critters the perfect addition to your family.

Get ready to fall in love with the fascinating world of hamsters—**we know we certainly have!**

YUP...

I'M **HAM-SOME!**

MEET THE HAMSTER

FURRY, SLEEPY, AND ALWAYS HUNGRY!

Hamsters are small mammals that belong to the rodent family. They're cousins of mice, rats, and squirrels. Like all rodents, they have large front teeth for gnawing and nibbling, and their teeth continue to grow throughout their lifetime! This is important because they are constantly chewing on hard nuts and food that would wear down their teeth otherwise. **Hamsters are quite the experts at munching on yummy treats!**

Hamsters are mammals, just like us humans. *So, what exactly are mammals?* Well, mammals are a special group of animals with a few things in common.

First of all, they're all warm-blooded, which means they can regulate their body temperature to stay cozy and comfortable. This helps them survive changing climates, and their bodies adjust in temperature automatically to stay comfortable.

Secondly, all mammals have fur or hair on their bodies. Some have short hair, some have long hair, and some have cool patterns like stripes or spots.

And finally, all mammals give birth to live young and nurse them with milk from their mom's special milk glands.

Some people think hamsters are ***nocturnal*** and most awake at night, but that isn't exactly true. Hamsters may not be nocturnal, but they sure do love their twilight hours! In fact, they are what are called "***crepuscular*** *critters*" because they're the most active during dawn and dusk. They are ready to have a hamster party when everyone else is just waking up or getting ready for bed.

This twilight-loving behavior helps hamsters avoid both daytime ***and*** nighttime predators. **That's right!** They get to play and munch on food without having to worry about any big, scary creatures trying to gobble them up.

But don't be fooled, hamsters can still have some bursts of energy during the day or night too. So, if you hear some rustling in their cozy little homes or see them spinning around in their exercise wheels, just know they're having a blast living their best crepuscular lives!

Here comes another surprising secret—although they may look like they love munching on veggies, hamsters are actually **omnivores** like us. Yep, you read that right! These tiny munchkins enjoy a varied diet consisting of plants, seeds, fruits, and occasionally, a bit of protein from insects. Most pet hamsters don't eat bugs, but in the wild, they wouldn't turn down a chance for a buggy snack.

Did you know that hamsters are expert diggers? In the wild, they create a series of burrows and tunnels to live and raise their young in. This is one reason hamsters love cages with built-in tunnels.

IT'S HAMMY TIME!

POPULAR HAMSTER BREEDS

MEET THE FURRY STARS OF THE HAMSTER WORLD!

Attention all future hamster experts! Are you ready to learn about the world of pet hamsters? Well, you've come to the right place! We're here to give you a rundown on all the different types of hamsters that can become your new furry friend.

Let's explore the delightful characteristics of each hamster breed, from the Syrian hamster, renowned for its majestic golden coat, to the speedy Roborovski Dwarf hamster, who is always on the move like a ninja. We guarantee that by the end of this journey, your love for these pint-sized pets will grow faster than their teeny-tiny feet can scurry within their hamster wheels!

SYRIAN HAMSTERS

Oh, the extraordinary Syrian hamster! These fluffy friends are also known as "*fancy hamsters*" if they have short hair, and "*teddy bear hamsters*" if they have long hair. They're the most popular of all pet hamster breeds. *Why?* Well, they're great for handling; they're pretty slow and not as likely to bite. But remember, they like living alone, so don't keep more than one in a cage!

This breed is large and can be pretty fuzzy if long-haired. They are also known as golden hamsters because their common fur color is golden yellowish-brown. Golden hamsters often have darker stripes on the sides of their face. But even though this is a common color, Syrian hamsters can come in various colors such as black, chocolate, grey, white, and many other shades. They can also have different patterns, such as a band of color around their middle, or they can be solid or even spotted with different colors.

Syrian hamsters are one of the larger breeds, and they can grow up to 6 inches long! Like other breeds, Syrian hamsters are playful and a very popular pet choice. They are fun to keep, and they love to roll around inside their hamster balls exploring their environment.

DWARF HAMSTERS

Get ready to meet the little guys that pack a big punch—**dwarf hamsters!** These tiny pals are super small and super cute, and they'll surely win you over with their playful personalities. Dwarf hamsters come in several varieties, from the Russian dwarf to the Roborovski dwarf to the Chinese dwarf. Spotting a dwarf hamster isn't hard since they typically only grow up to 2 to 4 inches long as adults, which is quite a bit smaller than full-sized hamsters!

A common color pattern for dwarf hamsters is to have a grey or brown coat with a black stripe on their back, which makes them look like tiny race cars! But be careful, because they can be a bit faster and trickier to handle than Syrians. Don't let your dwarf hamster loose on the ground because grabbing them is like trying to catch a tiny speedy ninja!

Let's look closer at two popular breeds of dwarf hamsters.

ROBOROVSKI DWARF HAMSTERS

Like other dwarf hamsters, Roborovski hamsters are speedy and always on the move. They love playing around. Although they're quite small, they pack a punch of energy and will keep you entertained for hours. In the wild, they live in the desert of Central Asia. Sometimes their long name is shortened to "Robo" hamster, although there is nothing robotic about these furry little guys. They're also called Russian dwarf hamsters. Roborovski hamsters are less cuddly and open to being held than Syrian hamsters, but they are super fun to watch. Just don't take your eyes off them since they are the fastest of all the hamster breeds and the smallest at only 2 inches long! If you look away, they might pull a Houdini on you and disappear altogether!

WINTER WHITE DWARF HAMSTERS

The enchanting winter white dwarf hamster is another great dwarf breed to know. Despite their name, winter whites usually have a light gray/brown color fur for most of the year, and they aren't very fluffy. In the winter, their fur gets thicker, and their back fur can turn lighter. They usually always have white fur on their underbelly. Also known as Siberian or Djungarian hamsters, this breed has adapted to have a changing coat color in the winter to camouflage themselves better in the snow. They're kind, active, and perfect for kids, as they tend to be less prone to biting.

FUN FACTS ABOUT ALL DWARF HAMSTER BREEDS

Dwarf hamsters are full of energy and love to play. They're always on the move, running around their cage, climbing on their toys, and spinning on their wheels. Watching them is like having a tiny circus in your house!

One thing to keep in mind is that Dwarf hamsters are social creatures and like to live in pairs. Just make sure to introduce them slowly and carefully, and only keep same-sex pairs to avoid any unwanted surprises (such as baby hamsters... ***and lots of em***)!

So, if you're looking for a furry friend that's small but mighty, a Dwarf hamster might be the perfect pet for you! Just make sure to provide them with the right environment, care, and a hamster friend, and they'll bring you lots of energetic entertainment.

CHINESE HAMSTERS

Last but not least, let's say hello to the delightful Chinese hamsters! These cuties are known for their unique appearance, with longer tails than other hamsters. It's like having a little furry dragon as a pet! They may be shy at first, but with some love and care, they'll become more sociable.

But be warned, these hamsters are exceptional escape artists! They're always finding ways to slip out of their cages and explore the world around them.

It's like having a little secret agent as a pet! So, make sure to keep their cage extra secure, or you might find your Chinese hamster hiding in your sock drawer or under your bed!

Despite their sneaky tendencies, Chinese hamsters make great pets. They love to play, and they love to explore their surroundings. They're curious and intelligent and love to climb, dig, and run around their cage.

So, if you're looking for a hamster that's both charming and adventurous, a Chinese hamster might be the perfect pet for you!

I LIKE THE WAY YOU

ROLL!

HOW TO SET UP A HAMSTER HOME

So, you've decided to welcome a hamster into your life. That's great! Setting up the perfect home for your new pet is crucial for their happiness and well-being. Lucky for you, we've got the inside scoop on how to create a cozy and exciting living space for your hamster.

First things first, let's talk about the essentials: **the cage.** While getting a cute, itty-bitty hamster house might be tempting, size does matter. As a general rule of thumb, the cage should be as large as possible to provide ample space for your hamster to move around and play. ***Remember, hamsters are small but active!***

We recommend a spacious abode—with at least 600 square inches of floor space—to give your hamster room to roam, explore, and burrow to their heart's content. This works out to a cage that is about 30 inches long and 20 inches wide. *After all, who doesn't love a good room upgrade?* The cage should also be at least 12 inches tall to allow for climbing and provide enough space for toys, food, and water.

Tanks, solid-bottomed wire cages, and glass or plastic cages are great options. But always remember, the bigger, the better!

BEDDING AND NESTING MATERIALS

Now that we have the perfect cage, let's make it cozy! **Get ready to channel your inner interior designer—*hamster style!***

Hamsters enjoy burrowing and nesting, so it's essential to provide soft, absorbent bedding for them. Avoid using wood shavings from cedar or pine, as they can be harmful to our little friends. Instead, opt for aspen shavings, soft paper-based bedding, or timothy hay.

Layer the bedding about 2 inches deep throughout the cage. Your hamster will have a blast tunneling through it. Don't forget to add some nesting material, like shredded paper or tissues, so they can build a comfy nest for snoozing.

PROPER VENTILATION

Let's talk about the importance of good airflow. Fresh air is crucial for keeping your hamster pal healthy and happy. A cage with a wire mesh or a tank with a mesh lid (as mentioned earlier) ensures proper ventilation. This means fresh air can properly reach their homes, and a comfortable, light breeze always flows through. Stagnant air can lead to a buildup of harmful bacteria, so let's keep those homes well-ventilated!

FOOD DISHES AND WATER BOTTLES

What to store food and water in is important. First things first, make sure your food dish is:

- A *sturdy* ceramic or stainless-steel dish that will not tip over easily. You definitely want something chew-proof. We don't want any choking hamsters!

- *Easy to clean* and small enough for your tiny friend to nibble at comfortably.

Next, you need a way to quench your hamster's thirst without letting water spill out and make a damp mess. The best option is a leak-proof bottle that attaches securely to the cage. Your hamster will know how to use it and will enjoy having a clean supply of fresh water whenever it is thirsty.

HIDEOUTS AND TOYS

Just like you, hamsters like to feel safe and secure. Give them a place to go for quiet time and to be able to hide when they feel overwhelmed by the hustle and bustle of everyday life.

Remember, hamsters are prey animals. When scared, a hamster's instinct will be to hide. Here are a few tips for picking a hideout that any hamster would love:

- Choose a *cozy* and *spacious* retreat, like a wooden or ceramic hamster house.

- Don't forget to add soft bedding to make their hideout extra snuggly and inviting.

Now, for the toys. A hamster's life can't be all about napping and eating; they need fun, too! Provide stimulating toys such as chew sticks, tubes, and ladders for them to play with. Adding toys will help make sure your hamster isn't bored and has a good quality of life.

HAMSTER EXERCISE EQUIPMENT

Hamsters may look a little *roly-poly*, but they actually have a lot of **get-up-and-go!** In the wild,

your hamster would need lots of energy to scurry around looking for food and running from predators. Luckily, your pet hamster doesn't have to worry about any of that, but it still needs to be active through running and exercise.

So, what exercise equipment does your hamster need? Here are a few great options:

- A *hamster wheel* is a classic choice. Make sure it's solid and safe for their tiny feet.
- Consider a plastic *hamster ball* to allow your little furball free-range exploration under your watchful eye. Just remember,

hamsters don't like to be rolled, even if they are in a ball! Let them control moving the ball.

- Don't forget *climbing toys* and *tunnels* to ensure your hamster gets to channel their inner acrobat.

And there you have it! Setting up a hamster habitat doesn't have to be complicated.

LOCATION, LOCATION, LOCATION

Where you place your hamster cage is very important. You need to find a spot that's not too hot and not too cold.

The first rule is to avoid placing the cage near windows or drafts. Hamsters don't enjoy sunbathing or spontaneous gusts of wind. Plus, constant temperature fluctuations make them feel like they're living on a weather rollercoaster—not fun!

Besides temperature, also consider how loud the place will be. Hamsters enjoy their peace and quiet. Try placing the cage in a spot that isn't too noisy or chaotic. Make sure the cage is far from loudspeakers or big appliances so your hamster isn't stressed by these loud noises.

Finally, make sure to keep the cage at a safe distance from any dangerous stuff, like wires or anything that can spill. Your hamster can quickly turn into a curious explorer if it ever escapes. And remember, if they can reach it, they just might chew it!

CLEANING AND MAINTENANCE

No one enjoys a smelly cage, this is also true for your poor hamster! *So how can you keep their home smelling fresh?* By having some furry friends like hamsters join your family, you'll need to add to your cleaning schedule. Just like with your bedroom, setting a time to clean can help make sure it happens. Here's a plan you can follow to keep your hamster's cage looking its best:

First, make sure you clean their food and water bowls daily. Next, focus on spot-cleaning the hamster cage every day. This means removing any damp bedding or waste that you can see.

Now comes the big clean-up! Once a week, you need to deep clean the entire hamster cage. This involves taking everything out, scrubbing the cage, and replacing the bedding. Here is a quick step-by-step guide:

1. Move your Hammy to a safe and secure temporary space, like an exercise ball or carrier.
2. Remove all the toys, accessories, and dirty bedding from the cage.
3. Using a mild, pet-friendly soap, scrub every surface of the cage.
4. Rinse thoroughly and let the cage dry completely.
5. Put in fresh bedding, toys, and accessories.
6. Finally, return Hammy to their squeaky-clean home!

Did you know that hamsters spend up to 20% of their time grooming themselves? That's right, they love to keep clean! But sometimes they might need a little help from us.

One way you can assist your hamster is by giving it a dust or sand bath. *Huh, cleaning with sand?* Yup, the sand helps hamsters get rid of oils and dirt, kind of like how we humans use scrubs. This is especially true for dwarf hamsters.

Simply place a shallow container with pet-safe sand into the cage for a day every so often. Make sure it is big enough for your hamster to roll around in, and that's it!

Long-haired hamsters might need some extra attention, as their fur can get tangled. Gently use a soft, unused toothbrush to groom them and make their fur shine. Remember to be gentle and patient, as they might get a bit ticklish!

With a sparkling clean cage and some grooming assistance, our hamsters will be the happiest and healthiest pets on the block!

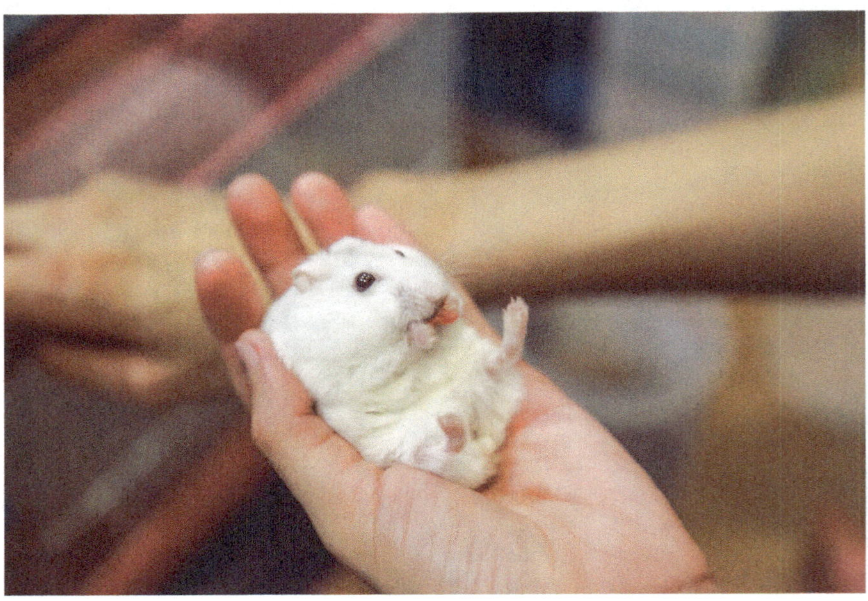

DETECTING POTENTIAL PROBLEMS

Now let's talk about detecting any issues that might come up in your hamster's home. If you notice funky smells or see your little friend's fur getting dirty, you've got to become a detective and find out why! 🔍

Smelly situation: If their home starts to smell, you might need to up your cleaning game or check that their bathroom corner doesn't need more attention. Remember, hamsters have a great sense of smell, so let's keep it fresh for their comfort too.

Dirty fur: If your hamster's fur gets dirty, it's probably because their habitat needs a good clean. Once you make their home spick and span, they'll be back to their fluffy and adorable selves in no time. Hamsters bathe themselves. If the cage is clean and you've already given them a sand bath, but your hamster still looks dirty, it may be a sign that your hamster is sick. It would be best to visit a vet to make sure everything is well with your little fluff ball.

THE GREAT ESCAPE - PREVENTING AND HANDLING RUNAWAYS

We all know that hamsters are curious little creatures who love to explore. However, their adventurous spirit sometimes leads them to try the "great escape" from even the coolest of cages. Let's talk about how to prevent and handle escapes.

First, always make sure your hamster home is secure. Checking that the cage door is closed properly and that there are no gaps or openings for sneaky escapes is an important step. If your hamster is a little Houdini, you might need to add some extra latches or clasps to keep them safely inside their cage.

However, sometimes even the best-intentioned owners come home to an empty cage. Even though your hamster is on the loose, don't panic! After you've cleared the area of any dogs or cats who might enjoy a hamster snack, take a deep breath. Here are a few steps to find your hamster on the run:

- Be quiet and listen out for their slight noises. Hamsters have a knack for finding tiny hideouts. Think like a hamster! Where would you go to find a hideout?
- Use a flashlight to search under furniture and in dark corners. Their beady eyes might reflect the light and give away their location.
- Set up some treats in various parts of the room. When your little fugitive gets hungry, it might be lured out of hiding.
- Place their favorite food near the cage. The smell of tasty snacks might entice them to return home.
- Remember to be patient! Finding a runaway hamster can take some time, and you don't want to accidentally scare them further away. If you aren't having any luck, wait until nighttime. Hamsters are crepuscular, so towards evening is when they will be most active.

Once you've found your tiny escape artist, it's time to carefully bring them back to their home. Use both hands to gently scoop them up, handling them with care to avoid bites or injuries (*remember, they might be pretty scared*). Finally, double-check the cage. Can you figure out how they got out to begin with? Make sure they can't immediately escape again!

In the end, having a secure, fun, and engaging hamster home will not only keep them entertained, but it'll also discourage your hamster from attempting any future jailbreaks. Happy hamster wrangling!

I CHEWS

YOU,

AS MY FRIEND!

WHAT TO FEED YOUR PET HAMSTER

Let's talk about what to feed your pet hamster to keep it healthy and happy!

Being an exceptional hamster owner means learning what your hamster needs to have a balanced diet. Thankfully, feeding your hamster doesn't have to be complicated thanks to commercially available pellet food or mixes with ingredients like oats, seeds, nuts, corn, and legumes. However, variety is the spice of life, and your hamster will also enjoy the occasional fresh produce, including fruits and veggies. Carrots, spinach, apples, and even seedless berries all make great treats. Just remember to keep seeds and pits away, as they can be toxic.

Just like us, hamsters need a balanced and delicious diet. This hamster food pyramid can help you ensure you keep their diet balanced:

- **Fruits:** Seedless apples, berries, pears, and more! This makes up 2-5% of their diet.
- **Vegetables:** Carrots, broccoli, cauliflower, and even cooked potatoes can make up 2-5% as well.
- **Grains, Nuts, and Protein:** High-quality hamster-specific commercial formula should make up 90-95% of your tiny friend's diet.

Remember, every hamster is unique, just like us! Always check with your hamster expert (or veterinarian) for the best diet plan.

THE IMPORTANCE OF WATER

Water is essential for your hamster's health. Here are some fun and important facts about water:

1. Hamsters need fresh water every day. Make sure to clean their water bottle and refill it daily!

2. Don't worry about how much they drink, just keep an eye on their bowl or bottle to ensure it's full.
3. Clean your water bottle frequently to make sure algae doesn't grow inside it.

OPTIMAL NIBBLING SCHEDULES

Our hamster pals love consistency, so you should set up a proper feeding schedule for them. It's best to feed them in the evening when they're most active. We don't want to wake them up during daylight hours for a snack, as they are crepuscular creatures. Remember, nighttime is their time to shine!

Here's a sample feeding schedule for our hamster friends:

- **Every evening:** Offer a small portion of hamster pellets and seeds
- **2-3 times a week:** Add some yummy fruits and vegetables to their diet
- **Once a week:** Surprise them with a tasty treat like a small piece of hard-boiled egg or a few mealworms

FOOD-TASTIC TOYS

Feeding your pet hamster doesn't have to be boring. There are food-based toys available that will keep your hamster entertained and healthy. They are especially a great option that stimulates their mind and takes care of them! Let's check out some great options.

CHEWS, CHEWS, CHEWS

Hamsters need to chew, chew, chew to keep their teeth in tip-top shape. Although they don't actually eat wood, hamsters love to chew on it! Try giving them wooden chew toys or wood gnaws—

they are the best option. You can even use pesticide-free fruit tree branches or hardwood blocks (as long as they're not chemically treated).

Oh yes, and cardboard! Hamsters can also chew cardboard pieces for fun, and as a bonus, it gives them a hiding place when playtime gets too intense. They love to go inside old paper towel tubes and chew on them. Remember to always provide a variety of chew toys for your little pal to prevent boredom and encourage healthy teeth.

THE TREAT-FORAGING MAZE

It's time to put on your creative hat and build an amazing treat-foraging maze for your hamster! This activity combines their love for food with their need for exercise and mental stimulation.

Start by hiding tiny bits of nutritious treats like spinach, broccoli spears, and dandelion greens throughout their cage and play area. You can even use small pieces of cardboard tubes or homemade tunnels to create a more challenging maze.

Watch your hamster have the time of its life searching for yummy treats while getting some much-needed exercise. Remember, a busy and entertained hamster is a happy hamster!

WHAT DO YOU CALL A MISCHIEVOUS HAMSTER?

Cheeky!

PLAYTIME SHENANIGANS

BONDING WITH YOUR HAMSTER

You will enjoy your hamster much more if you take the time to bond with it and hold it every day. In this section, we'll talk about how to bond with your hamster through playtime and training, all while keeping them safe and sound.

PICKING THEM UP SAFELY

First things first, you want to make sure you know how to pick up your hamster pal without causing them stress or harm. To do this, you must approach them calmly and gently, but confidently so they know you won't drop them or hurt them. Using two hands, gently scoop them up while supporting their bottom. It's best to pick up the hamster so they are facing you, making it less likely that they'll jump off since they can see what's happening.

TRAINING AND TRICKS: STIMULATING YOUR HAMSTER'S MIND

Hamsters are smart and curious, so keep their minds active with some training and tricks! Start by teaching them to come to your hand when it's in their cage. Offering tasty treats while calling their name will help them associate their name with something positive. **Remember to be patient.**

It might take your hamster a while to catch on, but they'll get there!

Once they've mastered coming to your hand, you can try teaching them some other fun tricks. An easy trick to start with is getting them to spin in a circle. All you have to do is hold a treat in front of their nose, say "Spin," and slowly move the treat around until they're spinning. When they complete the spin, give them the treat as a reward.

With practice, they'll start spinning on command and looking forward to their treat!

Another fun trick is teaching them to stand on their hind legs. You can do this by holding a treat just above their head, so they have to reach up and stand to get it. Say the command "Up" or "Stand." As they get better at standing, you can try having them do it for longer or even walk a little on their hind legs. Be creative, and always remember to reward them with love and treats!

WARNING SIGNS OF AN UNHAPPY OR UNHEALTHY HAMSTER

Sometimes your furry friend might not feel its best even with the best care. Let's look at some warning signs that your hamster might be unhappy or unhealthy.

Loss of appetite: If your hamster suddenly stops munching on its favorite treats, that can be a sign something is wrong.

Lethargic behavior: Hamsters are usually energetic balls of fluff. Napping even into the evening hours may be a clue that something is wrong.

Hair loss: *Hmm, patches of missing hair?* Hair loss is another issue that might signal something's off.

Ruffled or unkempt coat: A healthy hamster should normally sport shiny fur. If your hamster suddenly starts to look ruffled or dirty, this could also be a clue something is off.

Biting their cage: If your hamster gnaws on its cage like it's eating corn on the cob, it might be telling you its cage is too small or that they are bored and don't have enough to chew on.

Repetitive behaviors: When a hamster does the same thing over and over again, like constantly spinning around in its wheel and doing nothing else, it might be telling you that it needs more stimulation. Try to introduce new toys, teach your hamster tricks with treats, give it exercise ball time, or mix up the routine in another way.

Avoiding human contact: If a hamster that usually likes to be held suddenly starts acting withdrawn, or worse, biting when held, this could also be a sign it isn't feeling well.

To keep your hamster friend happy, make sure it has a nice-sized cage, different toys and exercise options, and most importantly, tons of love! Remember, it's always best to have your furry friend checked out by a veterinarian when in doubt.

I'M **FUR** REAL!

THE HISTORY OF PET HAMSTERS

TINY FURBALLS WITH A BIG PAST

Have you ever stopped to wonder about the history of hamsters? Where do they come from? What led them to become a popular choice for a pet? Well, we're here to shed some light on the origins of these delightful rodents.

THE GREAT HAMSTER REVOLUTION

In the 1930s, Israel Aharoni was a scientist who studied the disease leishmaniasis, which is caused by a parasite that is transmitted by sand-flies. He was looking for a new species of hamster that could be used for research on the disease.

Aharoni traveled to Syria, where he caught a few wild hamsters. He brought them back to his lab in Jerusalem, where he intended to use them as laboratory animals. However, he soon realized that the hamsters had a lot of potential as pets.

Aharoni began breeding the hamsters and studying their behavior. He discovered that they were social animals that enjoyed living in groups and that they were easy to care for. He also noticed that the hamsters had a lot of interesting traits, such as different colors and patterns.

Eventually, Aharoni sent some of his hamsters to a pet store in England. People loved the cute, furry little creatures, and soon hamsters were being bred for the pet trade all over the world.

Aharoni's work with hamsters also contributed to our understanding of genetics. By studying the different colors and patterns of the hamsters he bred, he learned more about how traits are passed down from one generation to the next.

LISTEN WHEN I'M **SQUEAKING** PLEASE!

THE HAMSTER LIFE CYCLE

Hamsters have a fascinating journey, from tiny pups scurrying around their habitats to grizzled veterans ruling the wheel with an iron paw.

From birth to old age, you'll learn the ins and outs of these surprisingly complex creatures - and maybe even chuckle a bit along the way as you discover the curious quirks that make hamsters such endearing pets.

FROM BABY HAMSTER TO FULLY-GROWN FURRY FRIEND

Hamsters are born very tiny, weighing between 0.07 and 0.10 ounces. That is only as heavy as a penny! Baby hamsters come into the world blind, deaf, and bald! But these baby hamsters, also known as pups, won't stay that way for long.

Hamsters can have varying litter sizes, but on average, hamsters usually have 6 to 12 pups. However, some breeds of hamsters may have as few as 4 pups in a litter, while others may have as many as 20. It's important to note that the size of the litter can also depend on the age and health of the mother hamster.

When baby hamsters are born, they only need the best meal for them ever—**their mother's milk!** This super nutritious liquid helps them grow strong and healthy. They'll enjoy this milk buffet for about 3 weeks, and then it's time to move on to solid food.

In their first few days, the pups depend on their mother for protection and food. They stay warm by snuggling close together, and you'll often find them all in a warm little pile.

Hamster puppies grow super quickly! In just two weeks, they'll start to look more like mini versions of their adult selves, with fur, open eyes, and even little hamster teeth. Hamsters are actually born with teeth, and they keep growing throughout their lives.

When the pups are four to six weeks of age, they become teenagers. At this stage, the teenage hamsters start developing unique personalities and are ready to explore the world. This is when they learn to play, explore, and get into the occasional mischievous antic. Males usually mature faster than females.

After 10 weeks, female hamsters can breed, and the circle of life continues. During adulthood, hamsters enjoy a balanced hamster lifestyle, complete with exercise, napping, play, and of course, snacking!

Hamsters reach their "golden years" at around 12 months, and on average, hamsters live for about 2 to 3 years, although some may live longer or shorter than this. While they may have a shorter lifespan, they sure make the most of their time.

FUR

BALL!

YOU ARE NOW A CERTIFIED HAMSTER EXPERT!

We hope you've enjoyed learning all about hamsters! Although there is always more to learn, you've earned the title of official hamster expert!

As you've discovered, hamsters add so much enjoyment to the world, with their tiny paws, twitching whiskers, and big personalities. They are truly fascinating creatures and make wonderful pets, especially if you want a late-night friend to snack with!

While you may be excited to own a hamster, it's important to remember that hamsters need proper care, including a clean home, the right food, and lots of love. So, if you decide to invite a hamster into your life, just make sure you're ready for the responsibility.

In the end, we hope this introduction to hamsters has made you smile and maybe even inspired you to learn more about these delightful creatures or even bring one into your home someday if you haven't already!

HAMSTERS ARE

SQUEAKHEARTS!

THANK YOU!

Thank you for reading this book and for allowing us to share our love for hamsters with you!

If you've enjoyed this book, please let us know by leaving a rating and a brief review wherever you made your purchase! This helps us spread the word to other readers!

Thank you for your time, and have an awesome day!

For more information, please visit:

www.animalreads.com

HAVE A

HAMSTERIFFIC

DAY!

ISBN: 978-3-96772-164-5

ISBN: 978-3-96772-165-2

ISBN: 978-3-96772-166-9

Animal Reads at www.animalreads.com

Published by Admore Publishing: Gotenstraße, Berlin, Germany

www.admorepublishing.com

Made in the USA
Las Vegas, NV
06 November 2024